ANATOMY AND PHYSIOLOGY:
Learning All About You For Kids

Copyright 2015

All Rights reserved. No part of this book may be reproduced or used in any way or form or by any means whether electronic or mechanical, this means that you cannot record or photocopy any material ideas or tips that are provided in this book

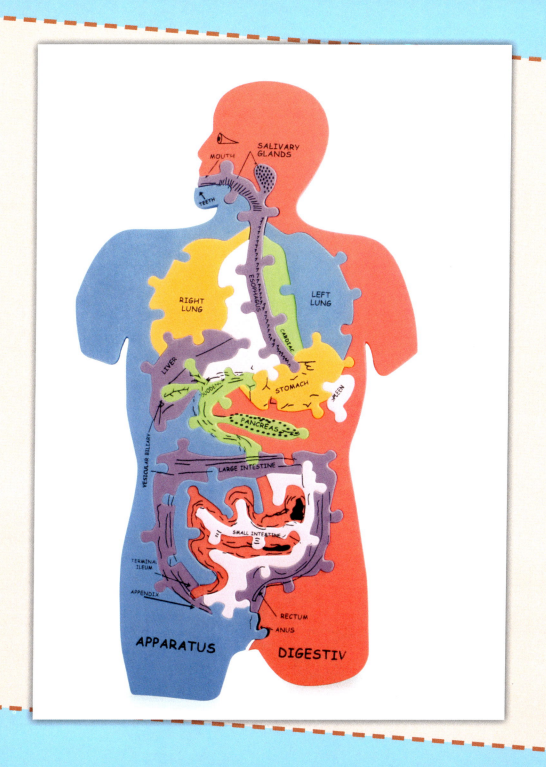

The Integumentary System

This system protects our body from various kinds of damage. The system comprises the skin and its appendages which includes the hair and the nails. The integumentary system has a lot of functions—it may serve to waterproof, cushion, and protect the inside tissues, excrete wastes, and regulate temperature, and serves as sensory receptors to detect pain, sensation, pressure, and temperature.

NAILS

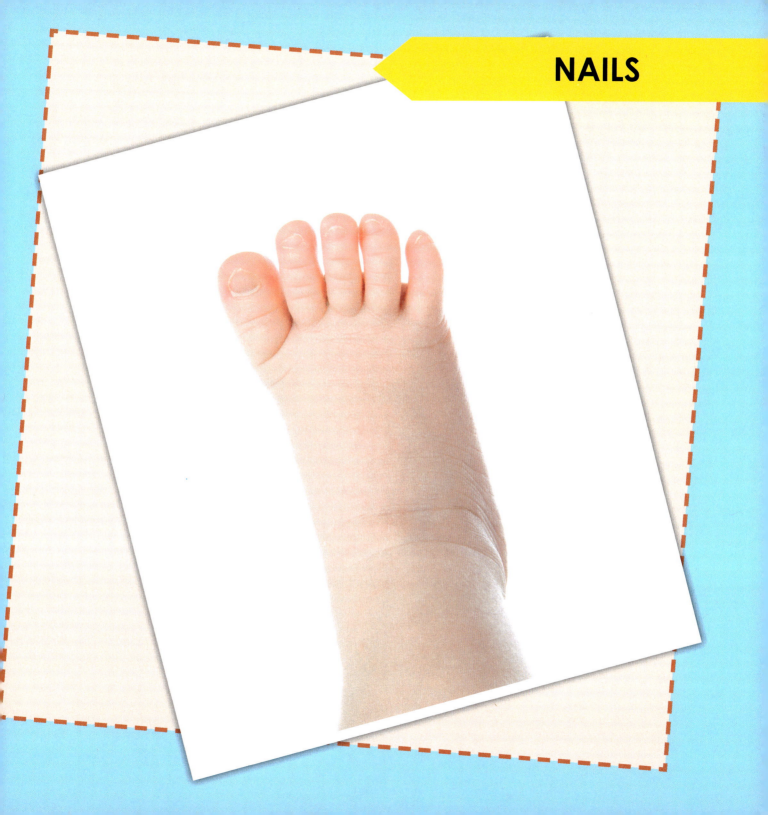

SKIN

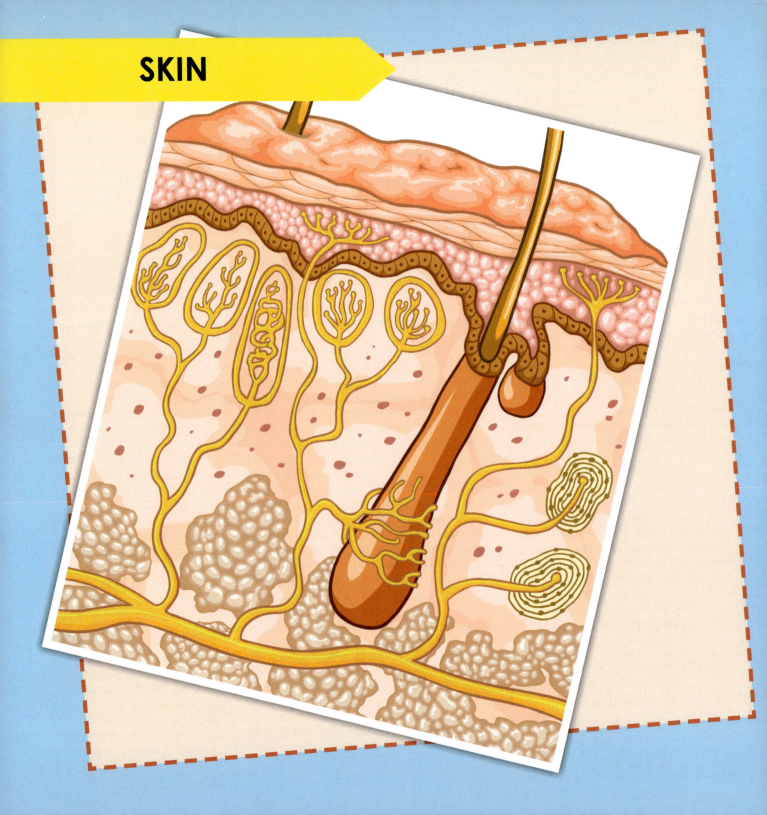

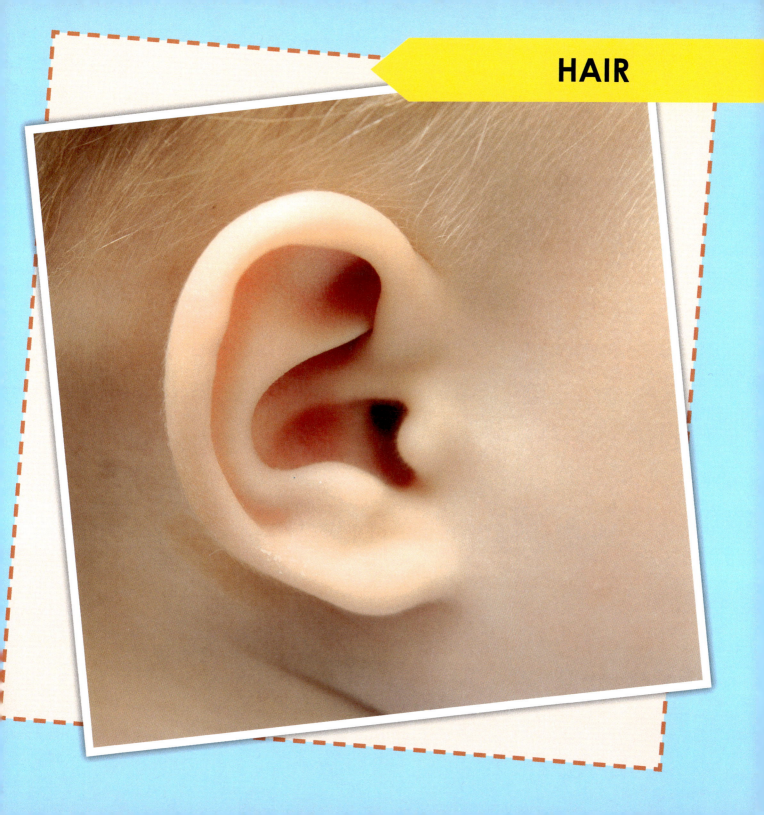

HAIR

The Skeletal System

The skeleton is the internal framework of the body. There are 270 bones at birth but decreases to 206 bones after some bones have fused together as we grow. It has six major functions—support, movement, protection, production of blood cells, storage of ions and endocrine regulation.

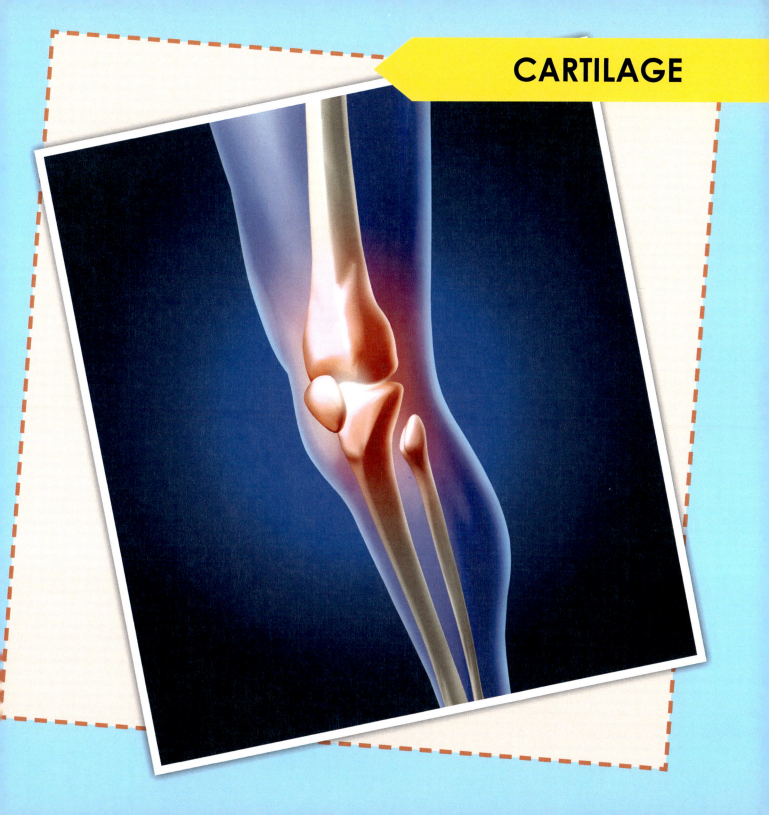

CARTILAGE

BONES

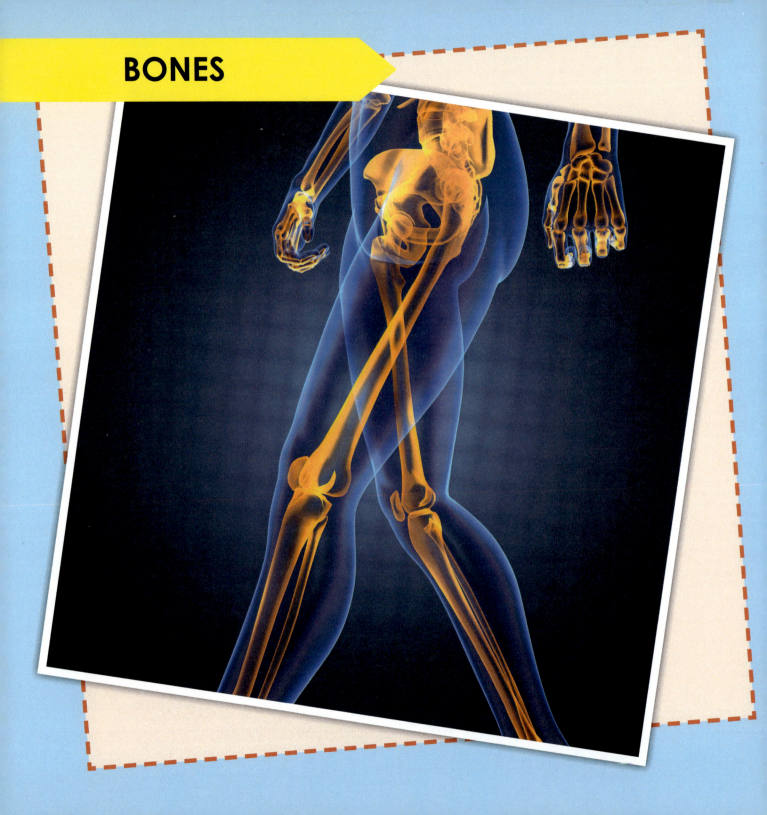

SKULL

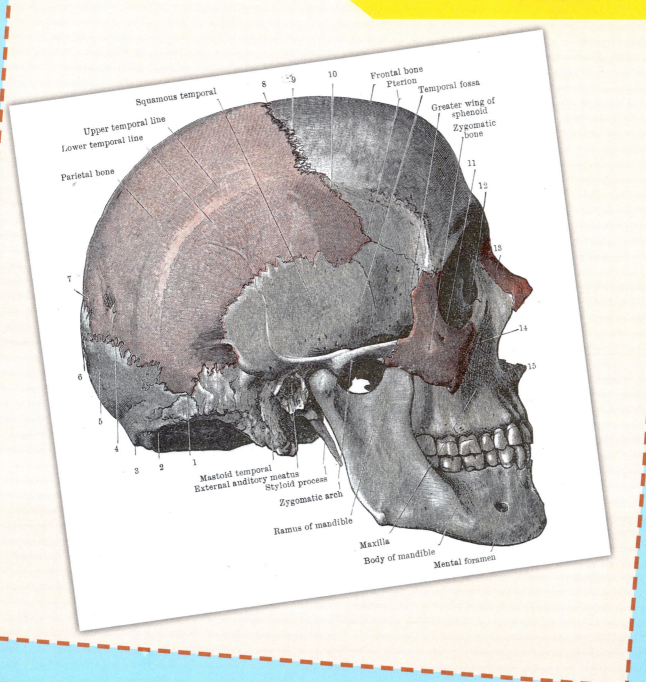

The Nervous System

The nervous system is the part of the body that coordinates its voluntary and involuntary actions and transmits signals between different parts of its body. It is consists of two main parts, the central nervous system (CNS) and the peripheral nervous system (PNS). The CNS contains the brain and spinal cord while the PNS consists mainly of nerves, which are enclosed bundles of the long fibers, that connect the CNS to every other part of the body.

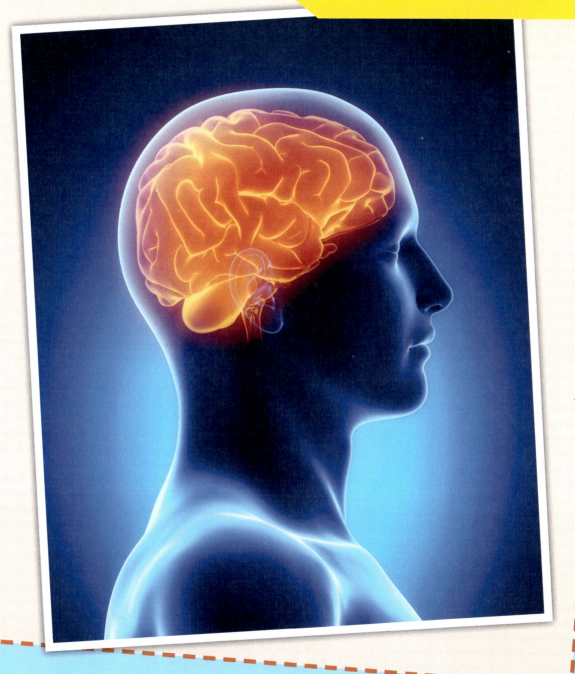

BRAIN

NEURONS

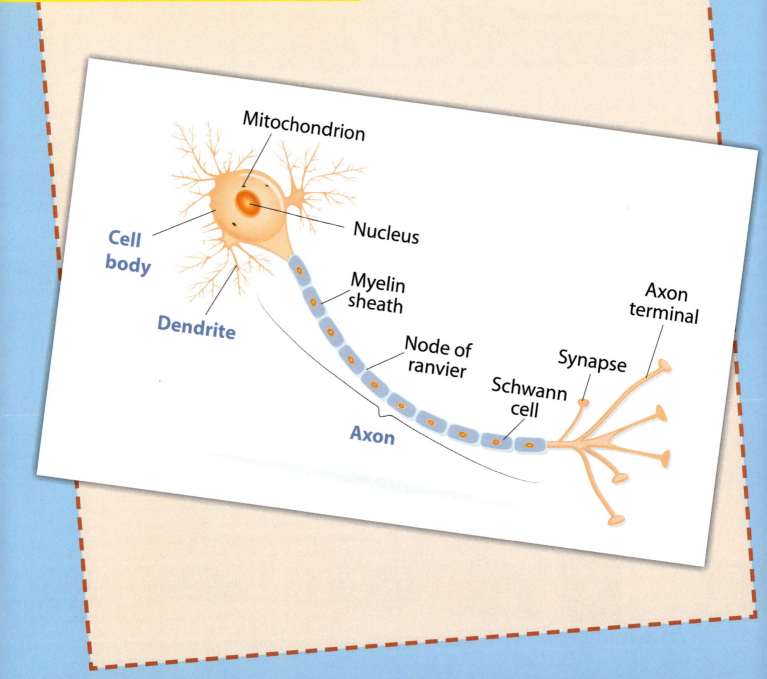

SPINAL CORD

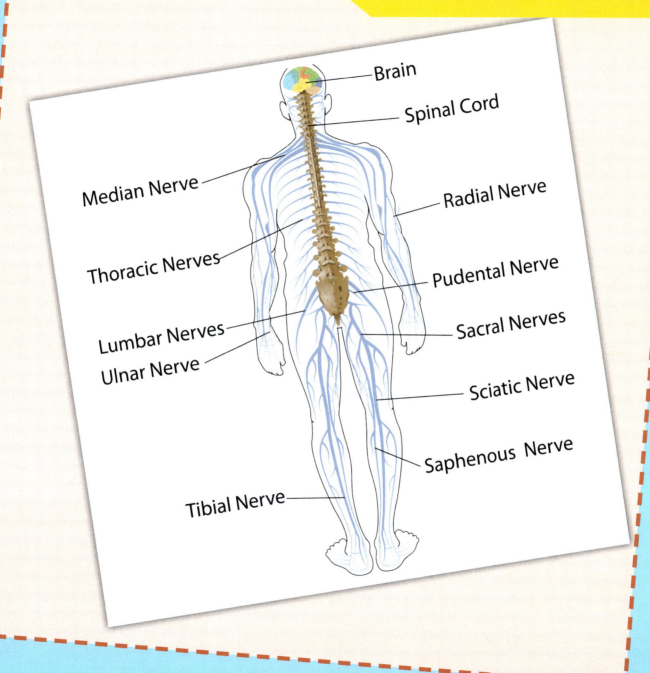

The Cardiovascular System

The circulatory system or the cardiovascular system, is the system that permits blood to circulate and transport nutrients, oxygen, carbon dioxide, hormones, and blood cells to and from cells in the body to nourish it and help to fight diseases, stabilize body temperature, and to maintain homeostasis.

HEART

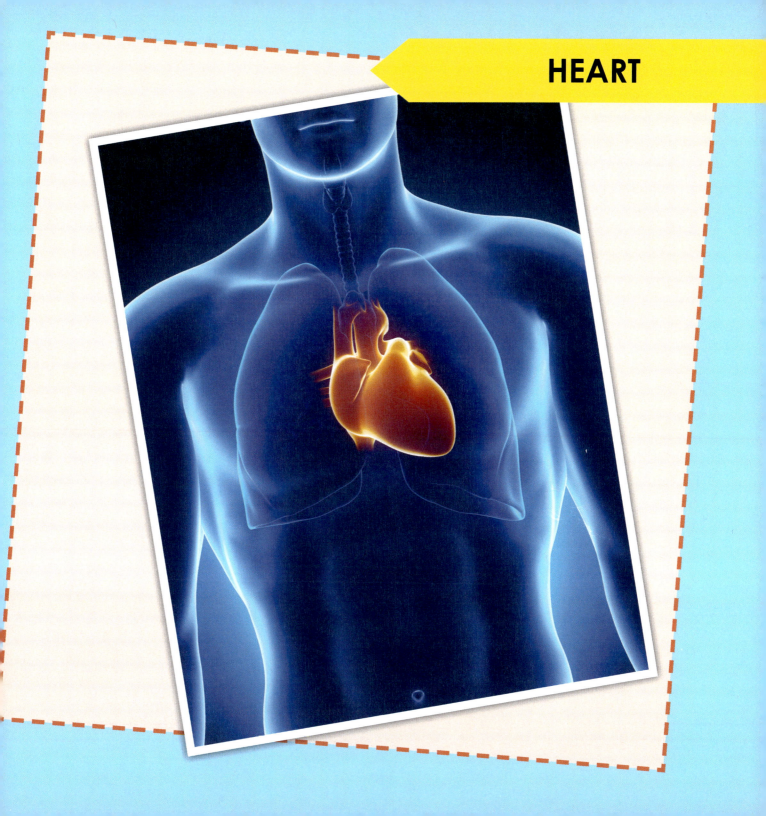

BLOOD VESSELS

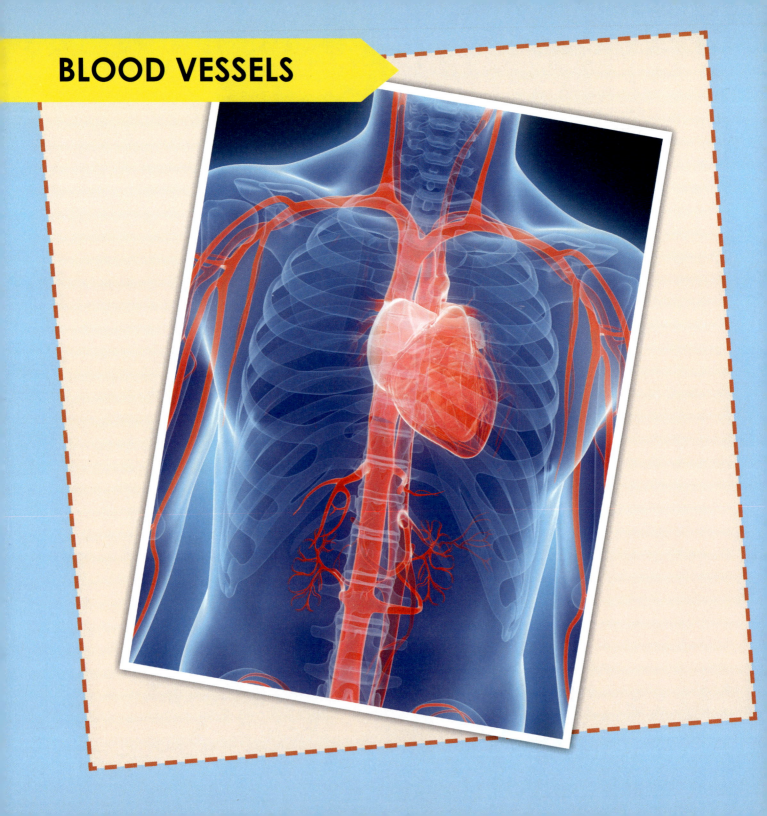

VEINS

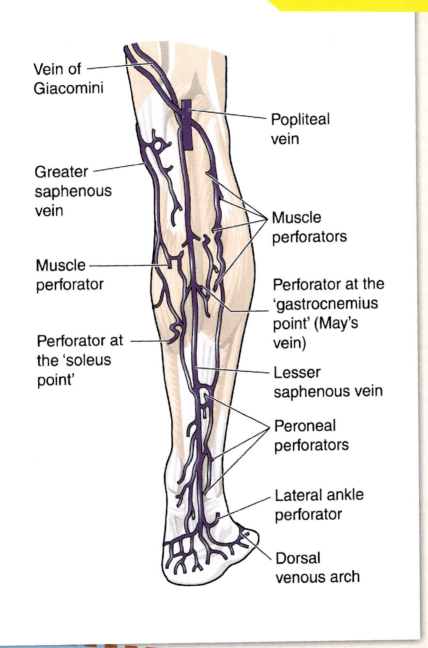

The Endocrine System

The endocrine system is the collection of glands of an organism that secrete hormones directly into the circulatory system to be carried towards a distant target organ. The endocrine system is different to the exocrine system, which secretes its hormones using ducts.

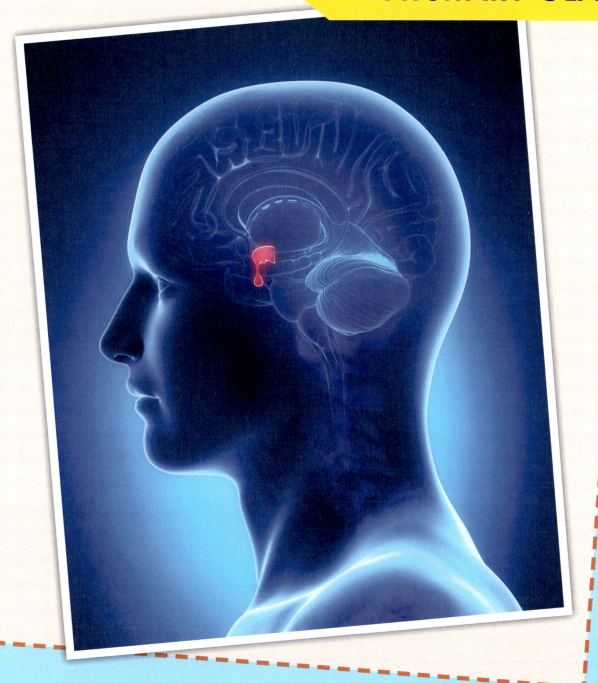

PITUITARY GLAND

THYROID GLAND

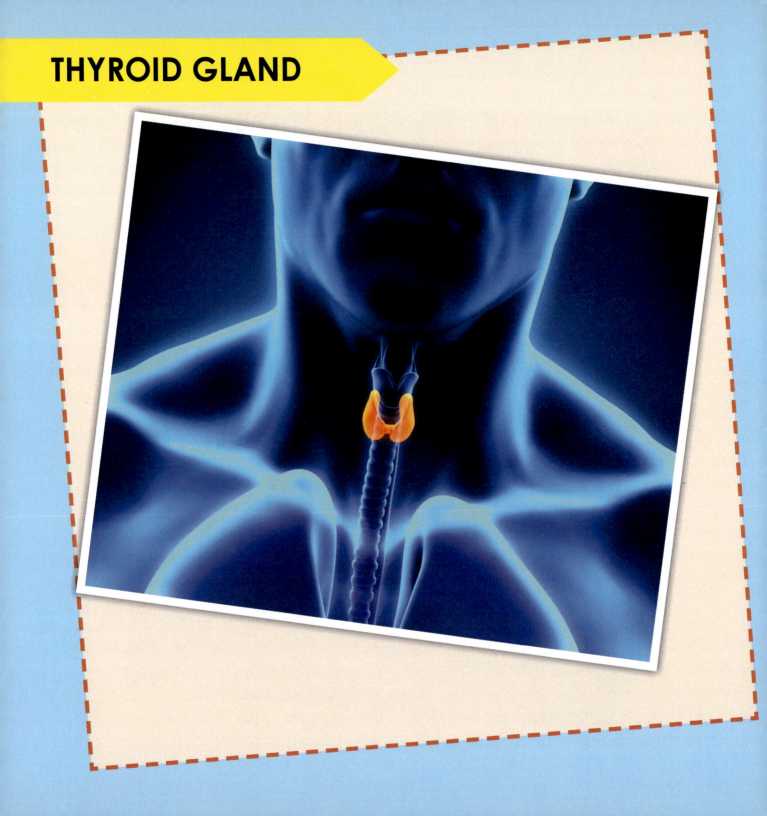

ADRENAL GLANDS

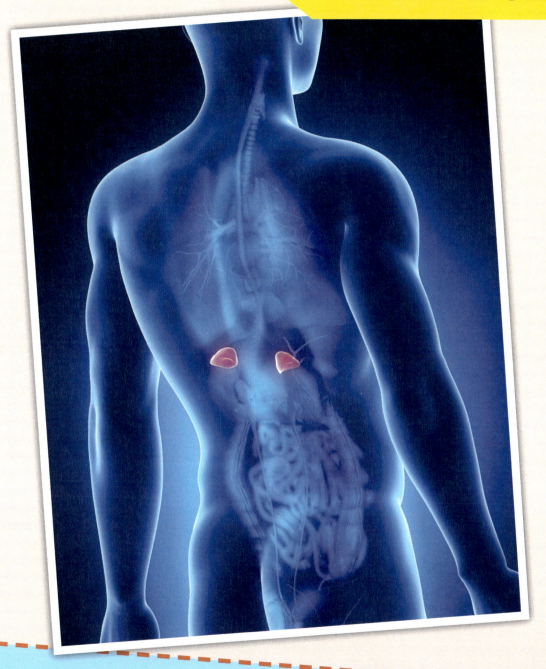

The Muscular System

This system consists of skeletal, smooth and cardiac muscles. It permits movement of the body, maintains posture, and circulates blood throughout the body. Together with the skeletal system it forms the musculoskeletal system, which is responsible for movement of the human body.

MUSCLES

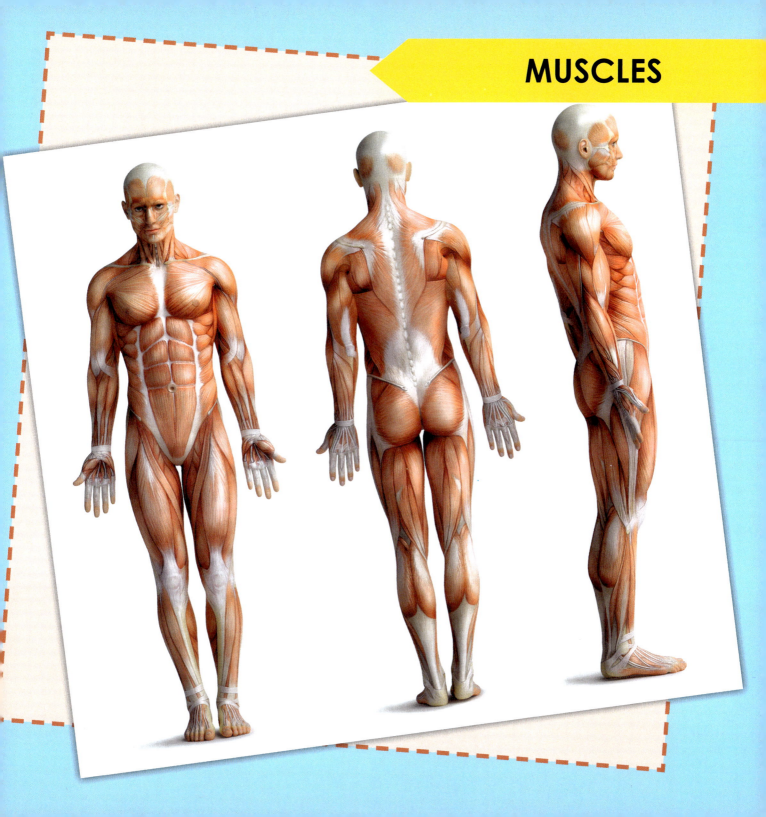

TENDONS

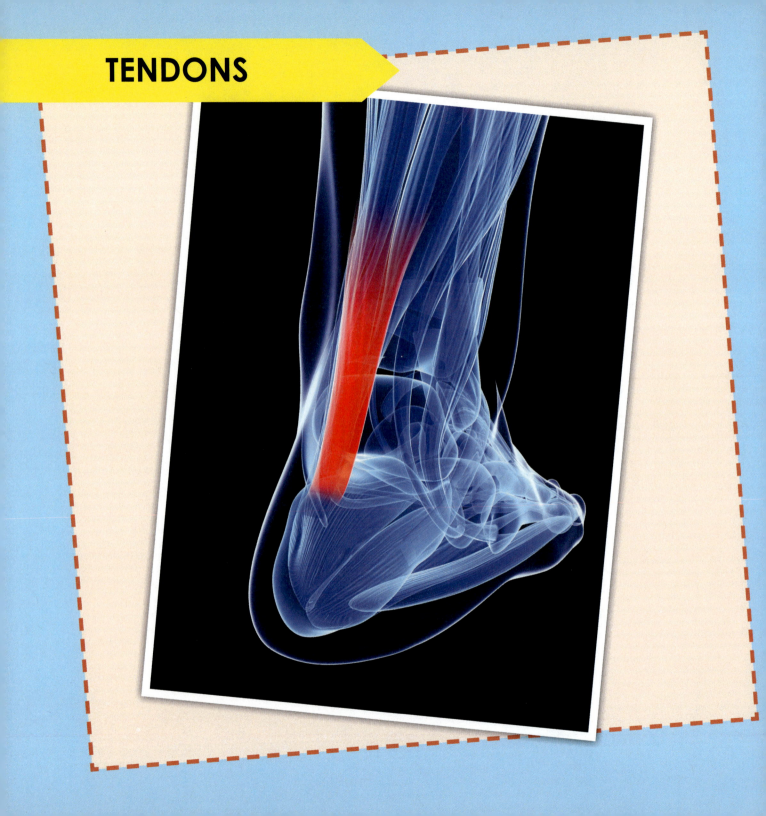

The Respiratory System

The respiratory system is the organ system consisting of specific organs and structures used for the process of respiration in an organism. The respiratory system is involved in the intake and exchange of oxygen and carbon dioxide between an organism and the environment.

NASAL PASSAGE

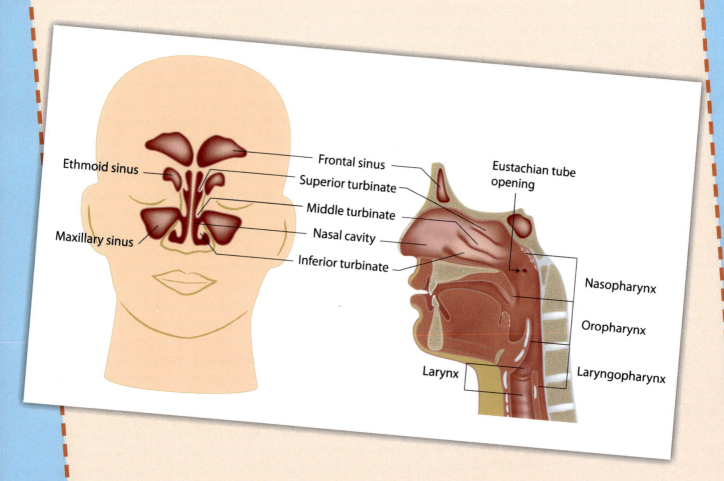

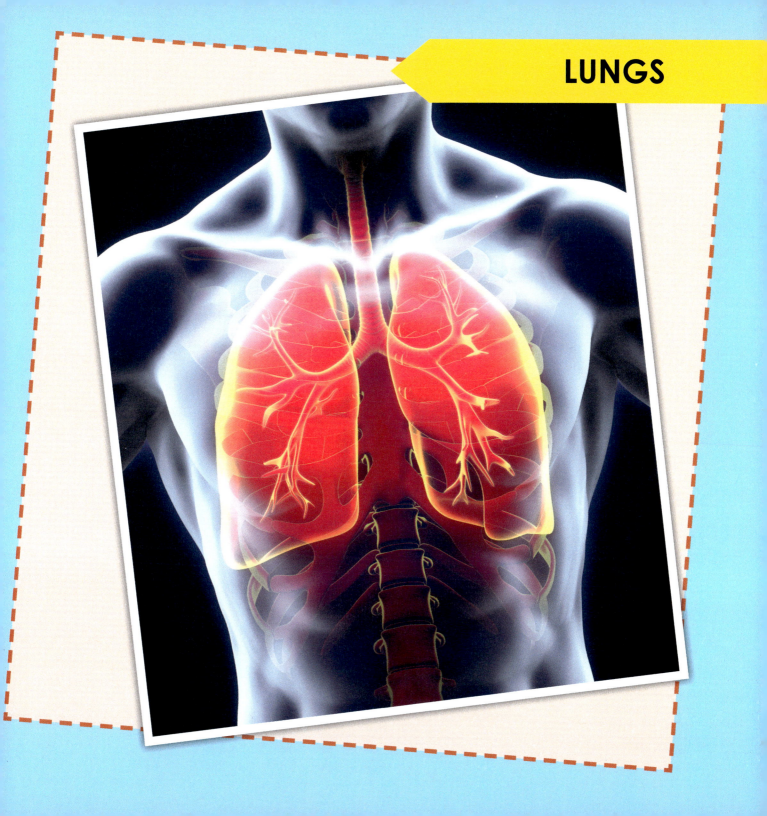

LUNGS

LARYNX

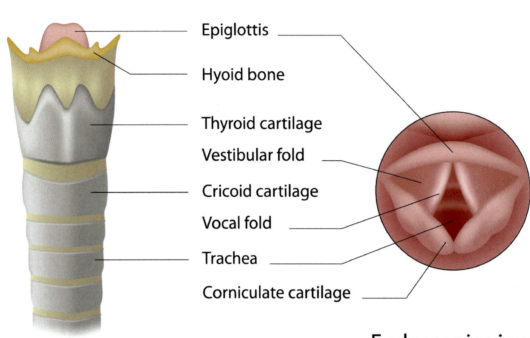

Anterior view — Epiglottis, Hyoid bone, Thyroid cartilage, Cricoid cartilage, Trachea

Endoscopic view — Vestibular fold, Vocal fold, Corniculate cartilage

Respiration

Phonation

BRONCHUS

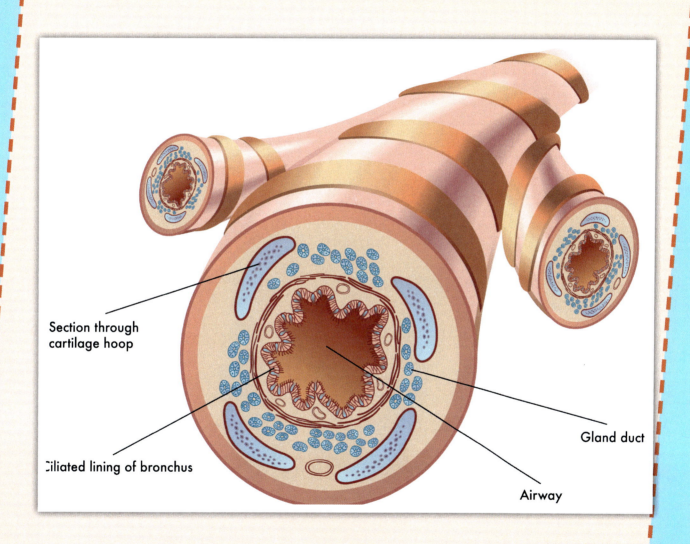

The Excretory System

The excretory system is the system that removes excess, unnecessary materials from our body fluids like urine and sweat, so as to help maintain internal chemical homeostasis and prevent damage to the body. It eliminates the waste products of metabolism and drains the body of used up and broken down components in a liquid and gaseous state.

KIDNEYS

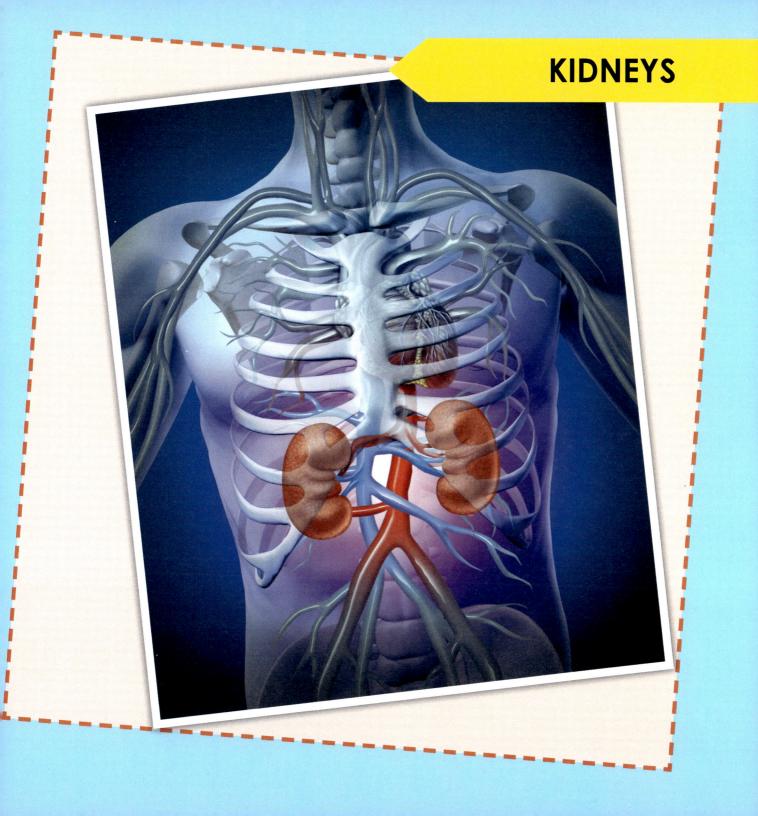

URINARY BLADDER

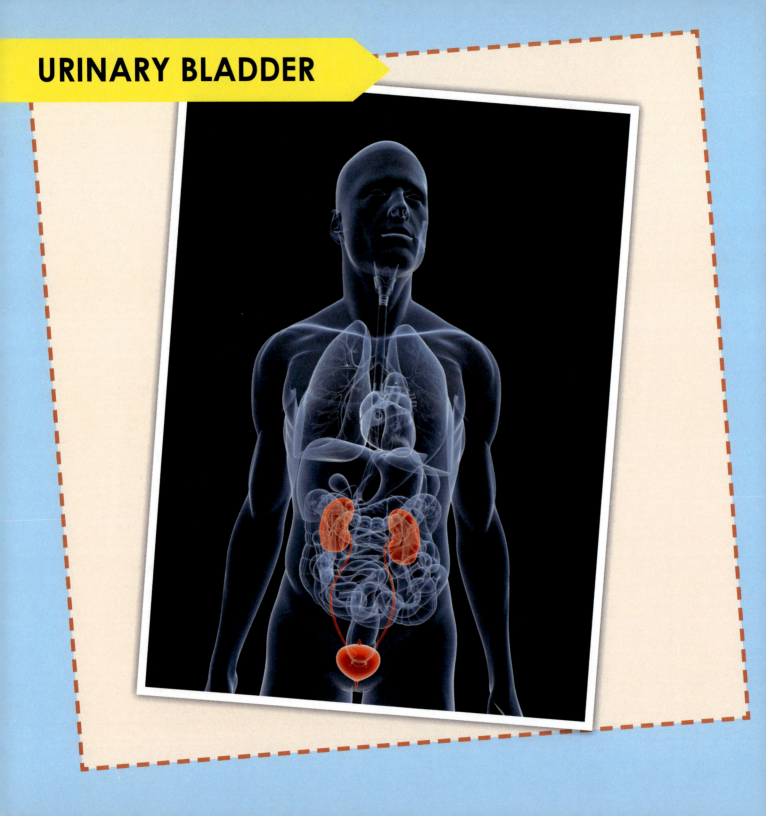

SKIN

The Reproductive System

The reproductive system is the system of sex organs which work together for the purpose of sexual reproduction. Boys and girls are different species that have significant differences including sex organs. With these differences, this allows for the possibility of greater genetic fitness of the offspring.

UTERUS

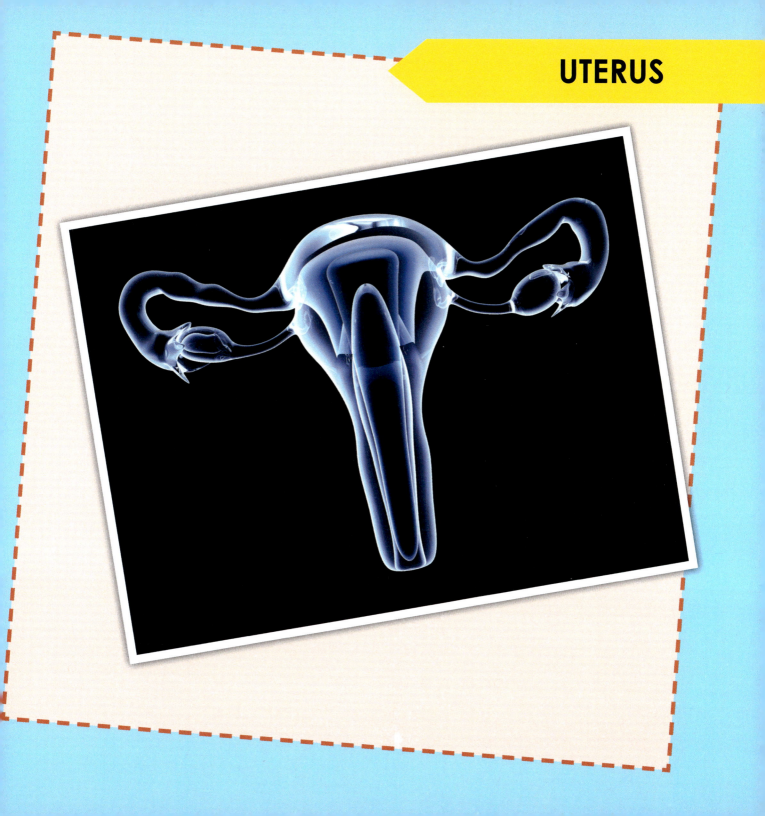

OVARIES

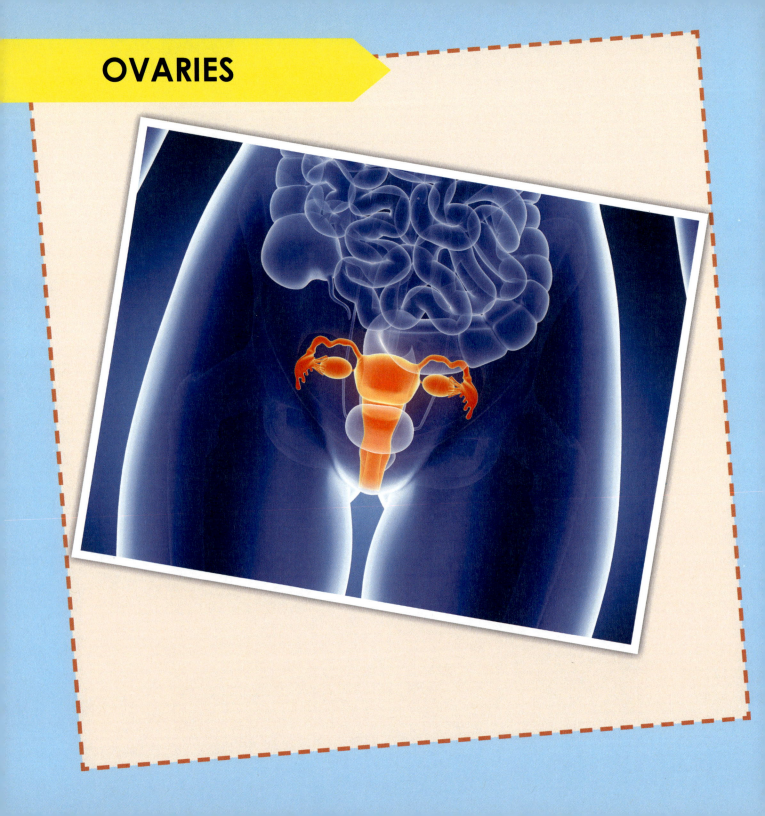

TESTICLES

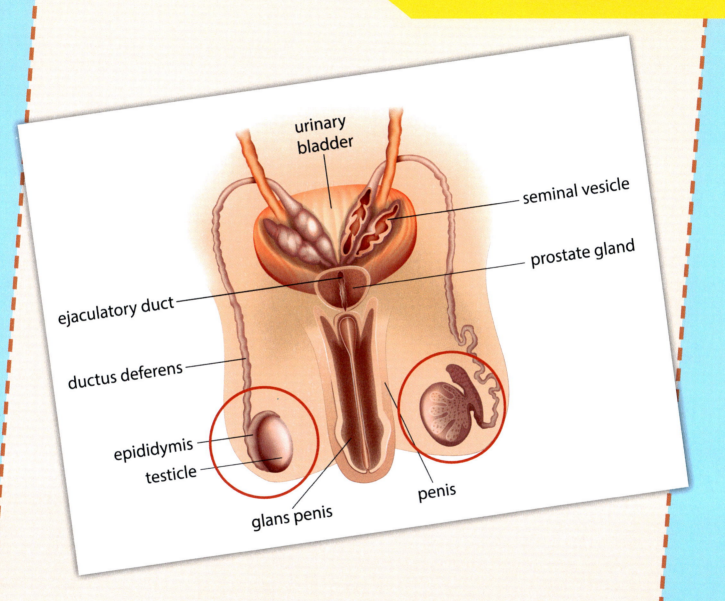

The Digestive System

In the human digestive system is the process of digestion. Digestion involves the breakdown of food into smaller (and smaller) components which can be absorbed and assimilated into the body. The saliva helps to produce a bolus which can be swallowed in the oesophagus to pass down into the stomach.

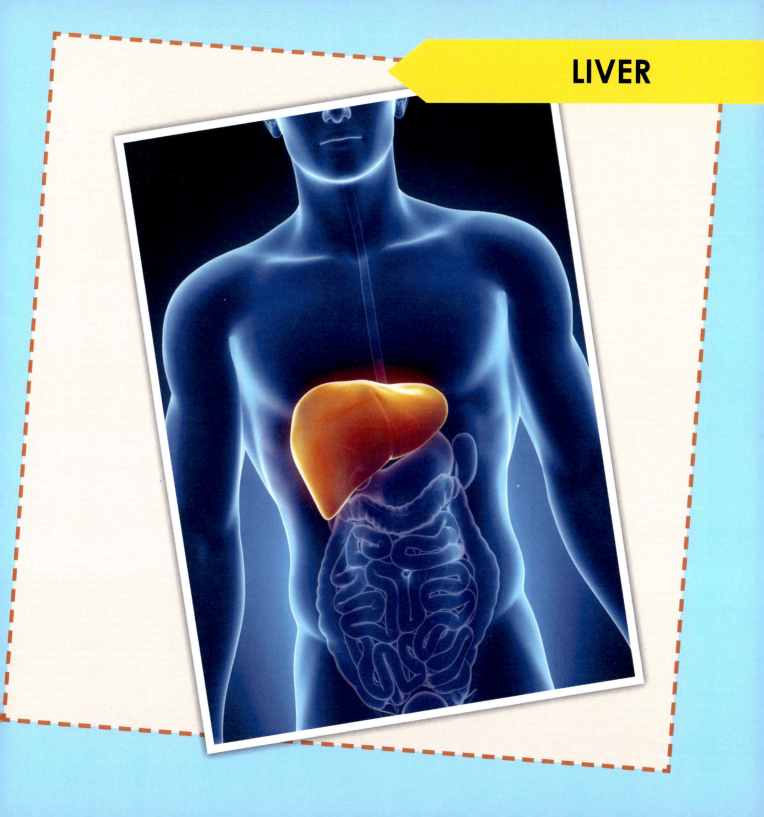

PANCREAS

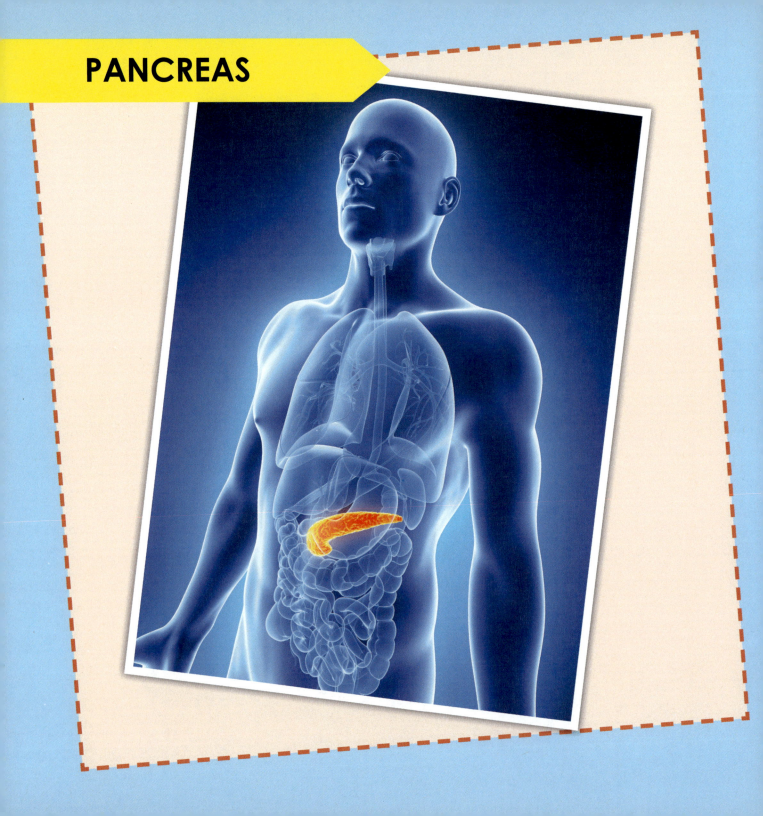

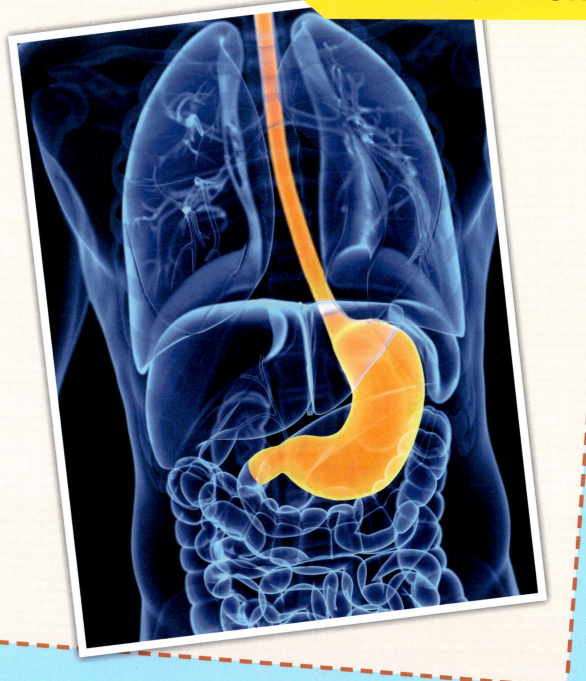

STOMACH

LARGE INTESTINE

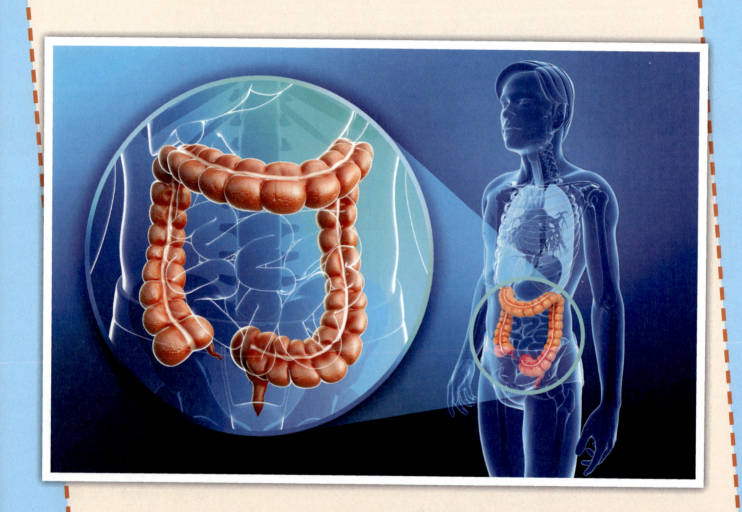

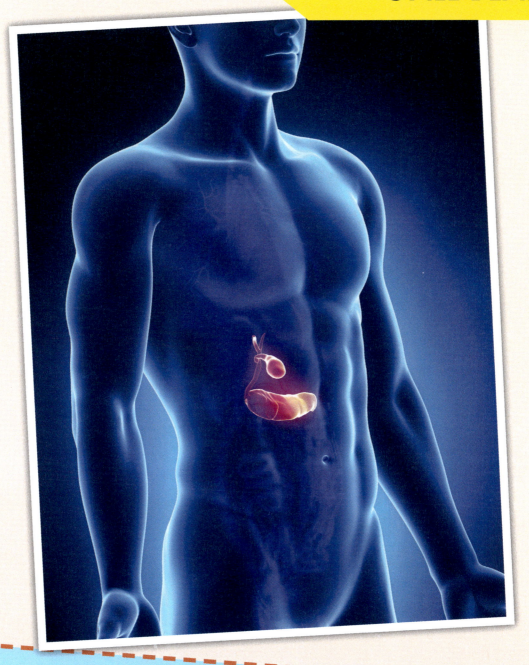

GALL BLADDER

SMALL INTESTINE

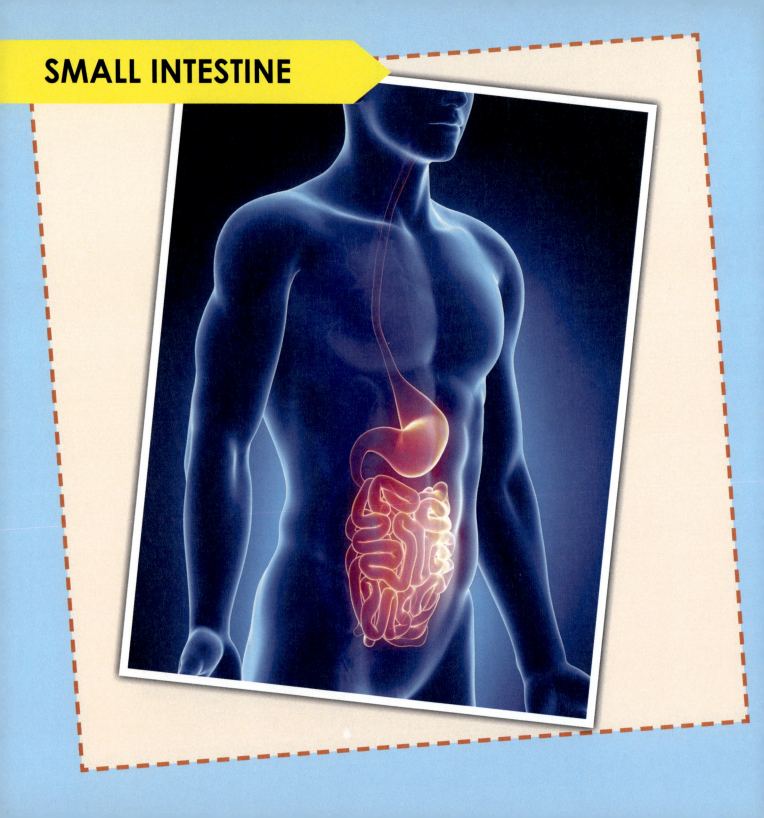

The Immune System

The immune system is the system that protects us against diseases. An immune system must detect a wide variety of agents, known as pathogens to work properly.

THYMUS

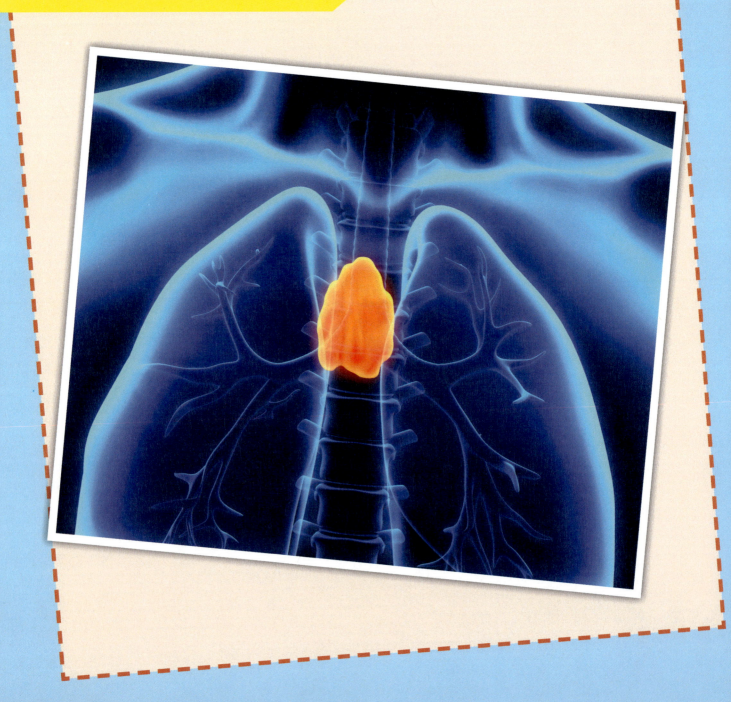

SPLEEN

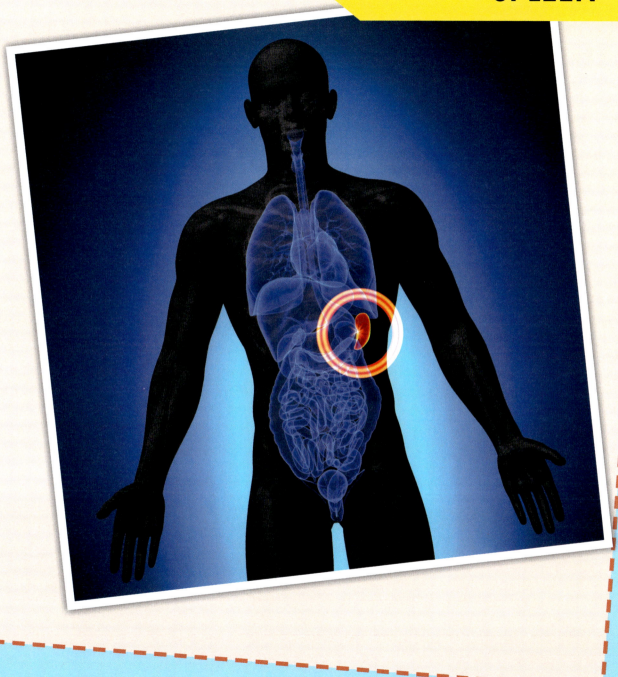

Made in the USA
Middletown, DE
15 August 2020